NATIONAL GEOGRAPHIC
PHOTOGRAPHY
GUIDE FOR KIDS

By Neil Johnson

NATIONAL GEOGRAPHIC SOCIETY

WASHINGTON, D.C.

J
77 /

For my children, Bradford and Hannah, who continually warm my heart and light my eye

Text copyright © 2001 Neil Johnson
Photographs (unless otherwise indicated) copyright © 2001 Neil Johnson

National Geographic Society
John M. Fahey, Jr., President and Chief Executive Officer
Gilbert M. Grosvenor, Chairman of the Board
Nina D. Hoffman, Executive Vice President, President of Books and School Publishing

Book Division
Kevin Mulroy, Vice President, Editor in Chief
Charles Kogod, Assistant Director
Barbara A. Payne, Editorial Director and Managing Editor
Marianne Koszorus, Design Director

Staff for This Book
Nancy Laties Feresten, Publishing Director, Children's Books
Suzanne Patrick Fonda, Project Editor
Bea Jackson, Art Director, Children's Books
John G. Agnone, Illustrations Adviser
Cinda Rose, Alexandra Littlehales, Designers
Meredith C. Wilcox, Illustrations Assistant
Melissa Ferris, Design Assistant
Deborah E. Patton, Indexer
R. Gary Colbert, Production Director
Lewis R. Bassford, Production Manager

Manufacturing and Quality Control
George V. White, Director
Vincent P. Ryan, Manufacturing Manager

Consultants; John G. Agnone, Peter K. Burian,
Tim Feresten, William R. Fonda, Charles Kogod

Library of Congress Cataloging-in-Publication Data:
Johnson, Neil, 1954–
National Geographic photography guide for kids / by Neil Johnson.
p.   cm.
ISBN 0-7922-6370-7 (PBK. ed.)—ISBN 0-7922-6371-5 (HC ed.)
1. Photography—Juvenile literature. [1. Photography.]
I. Title: Photography guide for kids.
II. National Geographic Society (U.S.). III. Title.
TR149 .J645 2001
771—dc21   00-012090

Printed in the U.S.A.

To learn how to
use a technique
called panning to
capture motion,
turn to page 62.

CONTENTS

INTRODUCTION

As far as the eye can see there are photographs waiting to be captured or to be created. Life swirls around us without stopping, but as a photographer, you can put a frame around moments in time.

A lot more goes into taking a good photograph than just pushing a button, though. You have to learn to use your camera, manage light, and work with your subject to capture just the right moment. This book will teach you the basics of using a 35mm camera. But its real goal is to teach you how to think like a photographer so that you can take great photographs with any camera.

You'll learn some of the tricks professional photographers use to create depth and texture and to capture motion. You'll also learn about the importance of getting to know your subject, whether it's a person, an animal, a landscape, or a building. Most important, you'll see how much fun photography can be.

Timing matters in photography. A split second sooner or later and the spray wouldn't be right in this girl's face.

All About Cameras

E very camera has certain features that set it apart from other models, but all cameras have these basic parts:

- a body (the lighttight box that supports all the other parts)
- a light-capturing system (film or a light-sensitive digital chip)
- a lens to focus the light onto the light-capturing system
- a shutter to control the amount of time light strikes the light-capturing system
- a shutter release button to open the shutter
- a viewfinder through which the photographer looks to compose the image

Most people use some kind of 35mm camera for taking pictures. Some kinds are completely automatic; some require that the photographer set all the controls; others are a combination of the two. Understanding what your camera can and cannot do will help you take better photographs. That's why it is important to read your instruction manual carefully.

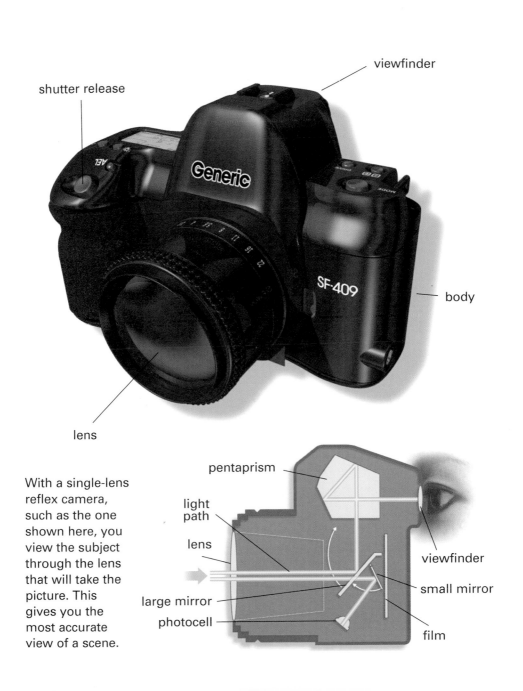

viewfinder

shutter release

Generic

SF-409

body

lens

pentaprism

light path

lens

large mirror

photocell

viewfinder

small mirror

film

With a single-lens reflex camera, such as the one shown here, you view the subject through the lens that will take the picture. This gives you the most accurate view of a scene.

KINDS OF CAMERAS

People who are interested in learning about photography usually start with either a disposable camera or a simple point-and-shoot camera (either film or digital) and then graduate to a more complex single-lens reflex (SLR) camera. Some of the advantages and disadvantages of each are described here.

DISPOSABLE CAMERAS cost very little because the body is mostly cardboard with plastic parts, including the lens. It will fit in your pocket and is easy to use. You don't have to worry about buying, loading, or unloading film since the roll of film is part of the camera. Some models come with a built-in flash. Others have a wide-angle lens for taking panoramas or are waterproof, making them great for the beach or pool. These cameras are perfect for when you don't want to have to worry about damaging your "real" camera or if you forget your regular camera. But you can't change the focus on a disposable camera, and the plastic lens does not create very sharp pictures.

POINT-AND-SHOOT CAMERAS are compact, reusable, and usually don't require a lot of technical know-how to operate. Most have a built-in flash, and many come with a zoom lens that ranges from wide angle to short telephoto. Most have automatic focus and other automatic features. Some models have fixed focus lenses; others have manual override, which allows you more control over exposure. Some expensive models even take interchangeable lenses. The lens the photographer looks through is separate from the lens that takes the picture, so framing is less accurate than with an SLR. But they produce clearer, sharper photos than disposable cameras.

SINGLE-LENS REFLEX (SLR) CAMERAS differ from other kinds of cameras in that with an SLR you view the scene through the same lens that takes the picture rather than through a separate lens. This means that what you see in the viewfinder is what you get in the finished picture. Whether manual or automatic with manual override, these cameras allow you to adjust the shutter speed, change the size of the aperture (lens opening), and use a variety of interchangeable lenses, separate flash units, and other accessories. Overall, SLRs allow you to be more creative with your photography. But SLRs are usually larger, heavier, more expensive, and more complex to operate than other cameras. Most people start with simpler cameras and "graduate" to an SLR as they become more advanced with their picture taking. There are digital as well as film SLR cameras, but digital models are quite expensive and usually are used only by professionals.

Note: A rangefinder is another kind of camera that, like the SLR, is fully controllable and that can accept interchangeable lenses. However, with a rangefinder camera, the photographer views the subject through a different lens from the one that takes the pictures.

DIGITAL CAMERAS operate in much the same way as other kinds of cameras. The big difference is that they don't use film. The light-capturing system is an electronic chip located behind the lens. The chip captures light as an image made of tiny dots, or pixels. This image is instantly displayed at the back of the camera. You can see the picture you have taken immediately, so it's easy to correct mistakes. Most digital cameras require access to a computer. They also use up batteries quickly.

FILM

Film, protected inside a canister, comes in rolls that are usually long enough for 12, 24, or 36 exposures. There is black-and-white negative, color negative, and both black-and-white and color slide film. Negatives are used for making prints; slides can be projected on a screen.

A color slide shows an image exactly as you saw it. In all negatives—black-and-white or color—the image is the reverse of what you saw. Dark areas appear light and light areas appear dark.

Color film is composed of three layers of dye: red, blue, and green. In the developing process, these three dyes produce all the colors the camera saw.

Over time, film goes bad just as food does. Be sure to check the expiration date on the box before you load a roll of film in your camera. If the film is out of date, its color may no longer be true. Film doesn't like heat or humidity either, so keep it in a cool, dry place.

Film for 35mm cameras produces either negatives (top left) or slides (top right). A memory card (bottom) records images in some digital cameras.

BLACK-AND-WHITE VS. COLOR

Most people prefer color film. After all, we see in color, and we live in a very colorful world. Color photography is so common that it is easy to forget that there is a second choice: black-and-white. A black-and-white photo can give a subject an abstract or timeless quality. Taking pictures in black-and-white can be fun, especially if you have access to a darkroom where you can develop your own photographs. Printing your own pictures gives you more control over the quality of the final image. If properly developed, black-and-white prints won't fade as quickly as color prints.

You can achieve strong photographs with either color or black-and-white film, but the mood created by each is different.

FILM SPEED

Film speed is a measure of how sensitive the film is to light. This sensitivity is indicated on the film box and canister by an ISO number (100, 200, 400, etc). In some cameras, you must tell the camera what speed film you have loaded by setting the ISO number. Many new cameras set the speed automatically by reading what is called a DX code on the canister. The lower the ISO number, the less sensitive the film is to light and the longer the shutter must stay open to expose the film. Conversely, the higher the number, the more sensitive the film is to light and the less time the shutter must stay open to expose the film. Slower film (ISO 100) is recommended in bright light, such as outdoors on a sunny day. Use faster film (ISO 400 or higher) for indoor shooting without flash or for shooting outdoors on overcast days. Fast film is also good for shooting active subjects such as sports or pets, because the faster the film, the faster the shutter speed you can use (see pages 24–25).

All film is extremely light sensitive. If you open the camera before the film has been fully rewound, you will ruin all of your exposures.

LOADING THE FILM

Follow the instructions that came with your camera to load and unload film. In many automatic cameras, the camera will wind the film for you and prepare it for the first shot. In manual cameras, you will have to wind the film until the number 1 shows in the frame counter. When it's time to unload the film, make sure that the roll has been completely rewound before opening the camera.

The silver and black pattern on this film canister is the DX code. This code tells the camera what film speed has been loaded and how many exposures can be made on the roll.

Make sure when you pull the film leader across the back of the camera that the edges of the film fit snugly onto the raised sprockets. Otherwise the film won't advance.

LENSES

A lens is a piece of clear glass or plastic that has been shaped to focus an image onto a piece of film or a light-sensitive digital chip. The size of the lens opening, or aperture, determines the amount of light that will strike the film. The quality of the lens determines the sharpness of the picture. That is why many photographers consider the lens the most important part of a camera.

Different lenses capture different amounts, or angles of view, of a scene. A normal angle lens is one that sees approximately the same thing as a person's unaided eye. A wide-angle lens sees a larger slice, and things in the scene look farther away. A long lens sees a narrower slice, and things in the scene appear closer. A normal angle lens for a 35mm camera is usually around 50mm. Popular wide-angle lenses include 24mm, 28mm, and 35mm. Short telephoto lenses include 85mm, 100mm, and 135mm. Anything 200mm or longer is considered a moderate or long telephoto lens.

Some cameras come with a normal lens or a slightly wide-angle lens. Most come with a zoom lens, which is like having several lenses in one. At the touch of a button these lenses move in and out to change the angle of view. An SLR camera (and a few other kinds) can be fitted with a variety of different lenses. That is why photographers often think of a camera as having two parts: a body and a lens.

Flash

Never touch your lens except to clean it. Use warm breath or a drop of lens cleaner and a special lens-cleaning tissue. Regular glass cleaner has ammonia, which will damage the lens coating.

24mm

35mm

55mm

85mm

200mm

300mm

These images were all taken from the same position with the same camera but with different lenses in order to show how the angle of view of a lens changes what is included in an image. The numbers beneath each image indicate the lens that was used to take the picture.

HOLDING A CAMERA

This picture shows the right way to hold a camera for horizontal shooting. Keeping your elbows tucked in will help steady the camera.

It is important to hold your camera steady. Put your left hand comfortably under the camera body. This position will support the camera and help keep your fingers from blocking the lens. Grasp the side of the camera with your right hand and place your right forefinger on the shutter release button. Use the same procedure whether you are right-handed or left-handed because virtually all shutter release buttons are on the right side of the camera. Press the button, using smooth, even pressure. If you punch or poke it, you will jar the camera and blur your picture.

It is not always easy to hold your camera steady. This is especially true if you are using a long lens or if you are making a long exposure in low light without a flash. If you are having trouble, try bracing the camera against something solid, such as a chair, a door frame, a tree, or a railing. Better yet, use a tripod.

Learn your camera controls by touch so you don't have to take your eye away from the viewfinder while you take the picture.

When shooting vertically, the left hand should still hold the weight of the camera. If the camera has an off-center, built-in flash, make sure it is at the top.

In low light without flash, you have to shoot at slow shutter speeds. To keep the camera steady, brace it on the back of a chair or some other solid object.

How a Camera Sees

A camera sees differently from the way people do. When we walk down the street, our eyes (and other senses) take in lots and lots of information—much more than we are even aware of—so we can interact with the world quickly and effortlessly.

But we don't pay attention to all the information our eyes take in. The mind focuses on the information it needs at the moment. You might be in a crowded room looking for a friend. Once you see the friend, your mind edits out all of the distractions. You look straight across the room, focusing only on your friend.

A camera can't do that by itself. It records everything it sees with equal importance. It is up to you, the photographer, to tell the camera what you want it to see so the picture you take shows what you want it to show.

By using a real window frame to create the illusion of a picture within a picture, the photographer illustrates the importance of telling the camera what to include.

2-D VERSUS 3-D

Because we have two eyes, we can see depth. This means we see in three dimensions (3-D) not two. If you cover one eye, you will only be able to see in two dimensions. The single lens of a camera acts like one eye. It cannot see depth. But there are a couple of techniques you can use to indicate distance or depth—the third dimension—in a photograph. One way is to show that things get smaller as they get farther away. This is most effective in wide-angle photos. Another is to emphasize the distance between the foreground and the background by adding something for scale. Yet another is to use light to create shadows that highlight depth, texture, and shape.

To see these 2-D images as one 3-D image, focus on the center point between the images and cross your eyes. As you relax your concentration, the two will "pop" into one 3-D image.

AUTOFOCUS LENSES

Most cameras have autofocus rather than fixed-focus lenses. This means that they automatically focus on whatever is in the center of the viewfinder. If you want something else to be in focus, you have to fool the camera. You can do this by using the camera's focus-lock feature. This is how it works: Move the camera so that the object or person you want to focus on is in the marked area at the center of the viewfinder. Slowly push the shutter release button part-way down to lock in the focus. Then, with the button still partially down, move the camera so the subject is where you want it in relation to the other elements in the frame. When you have the picture arranged the way you want it, push the button the rest of the way down. Your subject will still be in focus even though it is no longer in the center of the frame. This can create a pleasing picture design, or composition.

The upper photograph illustrates how a camera automatically focuses on what is in the center of the frame. By using focus-lock, you can focus on the anchor chain (lower image).

DEPTH OF FIELD

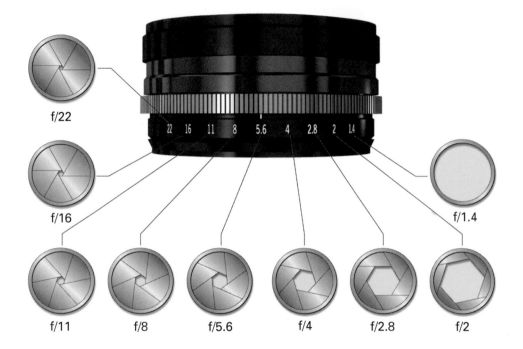

f/22

f/16

f/1.4

22 16 11 8 5.6 4 2.8 2 1.4

f/11   f/8   f/5.6   f/4   f/2.8   f/2

Aperture is measured by numbers called f-stops. This art shows how, with an SLR camera, you can control the size of the aperture by changing the f-stop. Each step of f-stop either doubles or halves the amount of light entering the camera.

Depth of field refers to the area of a picture that is in focus. If the depth of field is small, only the subject will be in focus. Anything closer or farther away will look blurry. When depth of field is great, the foreground and the background also will be in fairly sharp focus.

Depth of field is determined by three things: the size of the aperture, or lens opening (the smaller the opening the greater the depth of field), the length of the lens (the shorter the lens the greater the depth of field), and the distance from the camera to the subject (the farther you are from the subject the greater the depth of field). The more of these elements that you can use, the more control you will have over the depth of field in your pictures. For example, if you have a zoom lens and want a blurry background, move in close and zoom in tight on the subject. If you can set f-stops on your camera, you can increase the depth of field by selecting a small aperture (such as f/16) or decrease it by choosing a wide aperture (such as f/2).

 f/16

To show all three lacrosse players in focus, the photographer used a small lens opening to increase the depth of field.

 f/2

To show only one lacrosse player in focus, the photographer used a large lens opening to decrease the depth of field.

SHUTTER SPEED

Shutter speed controls the length of time the shutter stays open. It works with aperture to control the amount of light that enters the lens to expose the film or digital medium. Every camera except disposable or the very simplest point-and-shoot cameras have a light-sensitive chip that measures incoming light and automatically sets the shutter speed and aperture for the correct exposure. In an SLR camera the light meter may recommend a combination of exposure settings so that you can choose which is best for the picture you want to take.

To freeze this skater in midair, the photographer used a very fast shutter speed.

These two images show how shutter speed affects the way a camera shows movement. A fast shutter speed freezes motion (left), while a slow shutter speed blurs it (right).

Most of the time, the shutter is open for only a tiny fraction of a second, but there are times when it is open longer. The longer the shutter is open, the more blurred a moving subject will be.

Many SLR cameras allow you to choose the shutter speed. The camera then automatically sets the correct aperture. Fast shutter speeds (1/500 of a second or faster) allow you to freeze motion. Slower shutter speeds (1/15 of a second or slower) will show some blur. Some SLR cameras require you to set both shutter speed and aperture.

Flash

It is impossible to hold your camera completely still when using a slow shutter speed, such as 1/4 of a second. Brace your camera to keep the picture from blurring.

LIGHT

When lighting your subject, it is important to consider not only the direction of the light (front, side, back) but also the color of the background. Placing the yellow flowers (above, right) against a dark background, enhances the lighting and creates a more dramatic picture.

Taking a picture is all about capturing light. But there is more to working with light than simply making sure that there is enough of it to make a proper exposure. The quality of the light on your subject makes a big difference in the way the picture looks.

When a scene catches your eye or when a photograph in a book or a magazine impresses you, there is an excellent chance that the way the photographer used light is a big part of the reason. To take good pictures you must pay close attention to the light around you. It is always changing, depending on the time of day, the season, or the weather.

It is also important to notice how the direction of light affects the way the subject looks. Is it coming from in front or from behind? From above or from the side? What about the light source? How does a subject change when seen in sunlight, fluorescent light, or campfire light? Understanding how a camera sees light is an important step in learning how to see like a photographer.

Light does not always have to fall on the front of your subject. Here the photographer used the bright light behind the girl to silhouette her. The deep shadows in the tunnel create an interesting keyhole-shape frame.

DAYLIGHT

The brightness and the quality of light from the sun can be quite different depending on the weather. On a clear day, direct sunlight can be harsh. It will create dark shadows that can hide important details, but it will also give you bold colors. When you take a picture on a very humid day, the sun still casts shadows, but they are softer because the light spreads out as it bounces off the moisture in the air. This kind of lighting can give a photograph a certain moodiness that is absent in other atmospheric conditions.

This picture was taken at midday. See how the strong light makes colors bright but also creates dark shadows that hide features.

Overcast days produce soft light because sunlight is scattered by the cloud cover. The light comes from all directions at once, so there may be no shadows at all. Because there is no glare, cloudy days are excellent for taking portraits. Sometimes bright sunlight will give you the picture you want. Other times you will want cloud cover. The choice is yours.

There is an experiment you can do that will help you understand the difference between direct sunlight and overcast daylight. You will need a flashlight, any solid object, and a piece of white tissue paper. In a dark

These images were taken in two different kinds of daylight: in bright sunlight (left) and on an overcast day (right). See how the presence or absence of shadows changes the image dramatically.

room, place the object on a table not far from you and shine the light on the object. Notice that the shadow created is dark with sharp edges. Now hold the tissue halfway between the light and the object. Notice how much softer the shadow is. Think of the flashlight as the sun and the tissue as cloud cover.

If you don't want the harsh light of bright sunlight, move your subject into the shade. In shade there is light, but it is reflected light not direct sunlight.

You can learn a lot about the different types of daylight by taking pictures of the same subject at different times. Try photographing a subject at midday when the sun is overhead.

The color of light changes with the time of day. The higher the sun in the sky, the less atmosphere its light travels through so the brighter the colors look (left). At sunset (and sunrise) the shorter wavelengths of light (blues and greens) are filtered out, giving the light a warm yellow-red tone (right).

Then go back and take a photograph of the same subject when the sun is low in the sky. Try again on an overcast day and even on a rainy day. You'll be amazed at how different the same subject can look in different light.

By learning to use light and shadow you can add depth and texture to your photographs. Frontlighting—light that hits a subject head-on—tends to create a flat, two dimensional picture. When light strikes a subject from the side, it creates shadows that help define shapes and add dimension. If the sun is behind your subject, the light can create a halo effect around it. On very bright days, the subject may appear as a dark outline, or silhouette.

Reflected daylight can make a big difference. If you do not want dark shadows on one side of your subject, position it next to a light-colored wall so that light will be reflected into the shadows. But be aware of reflected color. If your subject is close to a red barn, the bright daylight will bounce off the red and give your subject a red cast on that side.

Shadows by themselves, such as the one cast by this boy against a red tent, can make interesting images.

Daylight coming through windows around the base of the dome in this cathedral brightens the area below but increases shadows in the dome.

INDOOR LIGHTING

Take a look around your house. During the day, most of the available light is daylight coming through the windows. Window light is a lovely light source, especially for taking portraits.

Window light can be very flattering for portraits so long as the sun's rays have been scattered by clouds or reflected into the room.

At night or in a room with no windows, light comes from an artificial light source. There are three main kinds of artificial light: incandescent (regular light bulbs), fluorescent, and halogen. Each of these produces its own color of light, and each color is different from daylight. That is why if you light your subject with light from a table lamp, you may get back a print that has a yellow-orange cast. If you take a picture lit by fluorescent lights, your print may have a greenish tint. A halogen light will give it a bluish tint. To reduce this problem, use flash and move close to the subject so it is lit by the white light from the flash.

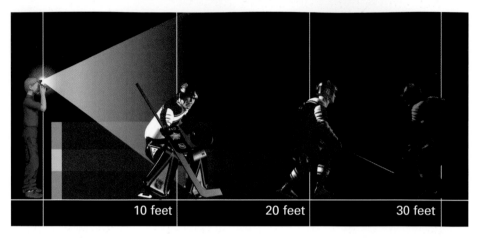

10 feet   20 feet   30 feet

This art illustrates an important fact: On-camera flash is most useful for subjects that are 10 to 15 feet from you. At 20 feet the light is 1/4 as strong as at 10 feet; at 30 feet the subject is almost dark.

FLASH

Many cameras have a built-in flash, but if yours doesn't, you may want to add a flash attachment to take pictures indoors or out. There are several ways to use a flash.

- As a direct primary light source. If you want to take a picture in very dim light, using a flash might be your best option. But direct flash light is very harsh. It tends to wash out people's faces and create dark shadows behind their heads.
- As a bounced primary light source. If you can adjust the direction of your flash, try bouncing the light from the flash off a nearby wall or ceiling. This will soften the light and make it look more like room light.
- As fill lighting. Bright sunlight can create deep shadows. You can use your flash to add light to these shadows.
- For correcting colors. Use the white light from a flash for more accurate colors in artificial light.

Remember, light from a flash loses its intensity very fast. By the time it is more than 20 feet away, it is too dim to be of much use. So don't even think of using it in a sports arena or concert hall. All your picture will show is the backs of the heads of the people in front of you.

When flash reflects off the retina, or lining at the back of a subject's eyes, it creates what is called red-eye. Some cameras have a device called pre-flash to help solve this problem. The camera flashes twice: once before the picture is taken and again as the picture is taken. The first flash causes the subject's pupils to shrink, making red-eye less likely. Another solution is to tell the subject not to look directly into the camera.

Red-eye can be avoided if your camera has a pre-flash feature or a flash that can be moved away from the lens.

These pictures were taken in bright sunlight. In the one on the right, the photographer used flash to fill the dark shadows.

Composition is the arrangement of the subject and its surroundings within the viewfinder. Composition has nothing to do with what kind of camera you have. It is all about what choices you make to create a well-balanced photograph. You must arrange the picture in the viewfinder so that it matches what your brain sees. Painters start with an empty canvas and add subjects. Photographers do the opposite. They include only those things that enhance the subject and avoid or delete things that detract from it.

As you explore the possibilities, ask yourself, What is the subject? How much of the frame should it fill? What is the best place for the subject in the frame? How does the subject relate to other things in the frame?

You can practice composing pictures by making a rectangular frame with your thumbs and forefingers. Looking through this frame with one eye closed is like looking through a viewfinder. Moving this frame closer to or farther from your eye is similar to using a zoom lens. Practicing composition with still subjects will make it easier to arrange things "on the fly" when you must shoot quickly.

By having this Halloween bear stand behind the fence, the photographer created the impression of a caged animal—and an interesting photograph.

The upper image has distracting elements. Notice how getting closer to the girls creates a livelier image.

MOVING CLOSER

Most snapshots show the subject and a lot more. Things are included in the frame that you didn't care about or didn't even notice when you took the picture. That's because the subject filled your attention—your brain removed or reduced the distracting elements. But your camera doesn't have a brain. It treats everything in the frame with equal importance. All the things that your brain tuned out are recorded in the picture, so it can be hard for someone else to tell what the subject is.

Nine times out of ten, simply moving closer to your subject will improve the photograph. Use your viewfinder to identify things that don't "help" your subject. Moving closer will remove these elements and allow the subject to fill the frame. If you can't get closer and you have a zoom lens, now is the time to use it.

BACKGROUND

Sometimes things around a subject help explain it. If this is the case, move back instead of closer. This will allow you to include more of the subject's surroundings. Let's say your dog has just dug a huge hole in your backyard. You could take a picture of just the hole or just the dog, but to tell the whole story, you need to include the dog and the hole. If you are photographing a treehouse, do you want to show the structure or do you want to include the whole tree so you can see how high off the ground it is? Again, the answer depends on what you want the picture to say. If adding background improves the picture, then by all means include it. If it distracts, then get rid of it.

Don't forget to pay attention to the position of elements in the background in relation to your subject. You don't want a flag pole or streetlight "growing" out of someone's head. Move the subject before you snap the picture.

Watch out that things in the background aren't "growing" out of the subject's head.

The cattle grazing contentedly help explain why this cowboy is taking a nap.

RULE OF THIRDS

The rule of thirds can be a helpful guideline for composing a visually appealing photograph. Making your subject the focus of attention does not mean that you have to put it in the middle of the frame. In fact, it often makes for a rather boring picture. Placing the subject slightly off center can help lead the viewer into the picture. It makes the subject seem less confined.

This is how the rule of thirds works. Pretend the viewfinder has a grid of tic-tac-toe lines. Place your subject where any of the lines intersect. Before you take the picture, move your camera around to find out which position "feels" most comfortable. Better yet, take several pictures with the subject in different places. Then review the pictures to see which one has the most appeal.

The off-center placement of this skier and the contrast between his angle and the angle of the spray heighten the sense of movement in this image.

VERTICAL OR HORIZONTAL

Because our eyes are positioned side by side rather than one on top of the other, we tend to view the world horizontally. Our brains let us see vertical things, such as trees and tall buildings, without turning our heads sideways. Cameras don't have brains. If you want to photograph a clown on stilts, you have to turn your camera vertically. If the camera has a built-in flash, remember to keep it at the top. Otherwise the lighting will be wrong.

But just because a subject is horizontal or vertical doesn't mean your camera position should match. Some subjects can be shot either way. Study the subject both ways through the viewfinder. Then decide which position best captures the image.

Shooting this gravestone horizontally shows its relationship to others in the cemetery. Taking the picture vertically isolates the subject.

N ow it's time to take what you have learned about your camera, lenses, light, and composition and put it all to use. There is a world of subjects all around you just waiting to be photographed. If the choice seems overwhelming, take a minute to think about what matters to you. Your family and friends? Animals? A special place? A certain sport or activity?

Once you have chosen a subject, try to figure out what it is about the subject that makes you want to photograph it. Take time to get to know your subject. This is just as important with landscapes as with people. The more familiar you are with your subject the more likely it is that you will be able to see the best way to photograph it. You will be ready to capture a special moment when it happens. Take lots of pictures—from near and far, from different angles, at different times of the day. This is called exploring your subject. Then look at your pictures and see which lighting, which angle, and which composition best shows off your subject.

Most of all, experiment! Be on the lookout for new ways to photograph familiar subjects.

To give this photograph a different point of view, the photographer crouched just inside the rear door of the recycling bin and aimed out.

PEOPLE

If you are like most photographers, you will take more pictures of people than anything else. Photographing people may seem simple, but there is a lot more to taking pictures of people than asking them to look into the camera and say "cheese." All that will get you is a face and a forced smile. A good photographer thinks about ways to capture a person's personality. This is easiest to do with people you know. If you are photographing people you don't know well, take time to talk to them. Be friendly, not pushy. This will help them feel more comfortable about having their picture taken. It is important to respect a person's feelings. If someone really doesn't want his or her picture taken, then move on.

When taking pictures of people, try to get them to forget about the camera and just go about doing what they enjoy (above and right).

PORTRAITS

With portraits, it's best to start with people you know. Think about what makes a person special, then pose him or her in a way that highlights those qualities. If your Uncle Bob always wears jeans and a cowboy hat, don't have him pose in a suit. Try to catch a natural expression, one that reveals something about the person. Not every portrait has to show a smile. Do you want the person sitting? Standing? Looking into the camera or away? Maybe the person would feel more comfortable doing

something he or she enjoys. If your father loves to cook, you might want to show him in the kitchen. Pay attention to lighting. Window light is nice for portraits. So is lamp light with fill flash. Don't forget to move in close. Fill the frame with your subject.

CANDIDS

With most portraits you have time to think about how you want a person to look, what kind of lighting is best, and so on. Candids are more spontaneous, which means you have less control over these things. You must be ready to snap the picture when just the right moment presents itself.

GROUPS

It is more interesting to pose groups of people in different positions or levels rather than in a straight line. The larger the group the more difficult this is to do. You might have some sitting on the ground, some on their knees or sitting on chairs, and some standing in the back. If there are some "stars" in the group (a bride and groom, great-grandparents) arrange the group around them.

Before you take the picture, remind the people that if they can't see the camera, the camera can't see them. Be sure to tell them when you are going to take the picture. "On the count of three. One, two, three." Don't forget to count loudly. Take several pictures so you can choose one where everyone at least has their eyes open.

Try to arrange groups of people in a way that shows they have a shared interest. Posing these kids so that they relate more closely to each other and the go-cart (below) creates a much more appealing image.

JODI COBB

"Always approach people with respect. Don't just snap and walk away."

Jodi Cobb was one of the first photojournalists allowed to photograph women in Saudi Arabia. Her sensitivity to the the country's culture and its ideas about privacy made it possible for her to take never-before-seen photographs of Saudi women. "Some women there had to get permission from their husbands or fathers to be photographed or they could risk divorce or loss of their passports." Being a woman can be an advantage in situations like this. "In many cultures women are more readily invited into the home."

Cobb says capturing people doing things they do every day makes for a more natural and lively photograph. She also likes to surprise the viewer. This photograph of a Saudi woman and two young girls at the beach speaks to both of these elements. It shows women enjoying more free-dom than they do in other settings. "Saudi women used to be completely cloistered. They couldn't go out in public unless they were com-pletely covered. Now they can go to the beach, but they could never wear a swimsuit. They have to swim fully clothed."

"Always allow people their dignity. The more time you can spend with your subject, the better your picture will be."

Beach scene, Saudi Arabia

TIP FROM THE PRO
Clip interesting pictures that you see in magazines
and ask yourself why you are drawn to them. Then
think about this when taking your own pictures.
Experiment. Use different lenses, change your
viewing angle, and try different lighting to go beyond
the snapshot or the cliché. Then study your pictures
closely and learn from your mistakes.

ANIMALS

Getting down to your pet's eye level and moving in close will improve your photographs of them. Don't wait too long, or you'll miss the shot.

In many ways, taking a picture of an animal is a lot like taking a picture of a person. Your picture should show something special about that particular animal. Spend time observing the animal before taking any pictures. You'll discover that, like people, animals have personalities and behavior patterns. The more you know about an animal, the better your chance of capturing an interesting pose. If your dog's favorite trick is to knock over the garbage can when he thinks nobody's looking, hide quietly nearby and wait for him to do it. If your cat loves to lie on a sunny window seat, try to catch her when the light is just

right. Get as close to the animal as possible. It's also best to be on the same eye level. In the case of your pet, this might mean sitting or lying on the ground. Try to avoid using flash. It's better to use fast film (ISO 400 or 800) or bright light.

If you are taking pictures of larger animals, such as a horse in a barn, you must be especially careful not to startle them, or you or someone else could get hurt. The animal may be easily spooked by a flash. If you must use a flash, try to get the animal used to the light and the clicking sound of the camera by taking several pictures near it before focusing directly on the animal.

It can be a challenge to take pictures at zoos and aquariums where the animals are behind bars or glass. Find out when the animals are most active—usually at feeding time and early and late in the day—and plan to visit then. Use your zoom or telephoto lens. Remember to place your lens close to any fence or glass so it doesn't show in the picture. Move around so that you can take advantage of the best lighting. If you have to use a flash and are shooting through glass, be sure to shoot at an angle to the glass so that the light from the flash doesn't bounce back into the lens and make a bright spot in the picture.

Your chances of getting a good photograph at the zoo will improve when there are baby animals or when groups are active and interacting. Be patient, and you'll be rewarded with moments like this.

Lion in sandstorm, South Africa

TIP FROM THE PRO

It is important to respect animals and not take risks with wildlife. To learn about a species, spend time with people who know about that animal. Get out of bed early. Adjust your schedule to the animal's.

CHRIS JOHNS

"The pleasure is learning about animals and letting them come to me."

Chris Johns was on his way to photograph meerkats when he first saw this lion. "It was around lunchtime when I passed a pride of lions in my Land Rover. The lighting was terrible, and they weren't doing much because of the heat, so I went on my way. Later in the day a thunderstorm developed. The high winds created a dust storm. I knew I had all the elements for making a dramatic photograph. I just needed the right subject. I remembered the lions and drove back to see if I could find them. This one male was walking by himself. He didn't pay any attention to me. All he wanted to do was get out of the storm."

Johns makes a practice of photographing animals more on their terms than his. "You have to get inside an animal's skin so you can anticipate their behavior." This takes a great deal of patience and persistence.

He is always trying to go beyond the obvious; to show something in a different, more insightful way. "A lot of your best photos are taken in the worst conditions. They give the photos an 'edge' they wouldn't otherwise have."

LANDSCAPES

The serenity of this bayou scene is enhanced by the canoe and its paddlers, who convey a sense of wonder and invite the viewer to follow them into the picture.

The first step in photographing a landscape is to figure out what makes that particular place so visually appealing to you. Is it the splash of ocean surf hitting the rocks under a cliff? A lush green fern bed under the towering trees of a forest? A red barn against the rolling hills of farmland stretching into the distance? Is it the way the dappled light falls through the trees onto a park bench; the odd angles of an old, falling-down shed; the busy geometrics of city buildings just as the lights come on at dusk? Do you like the way the wind is whipping the branches of a tree or the contrast of a red maple leaf against a black rock? If you can identify what you love about a place, then you can make that the focus of your photograph. Everything else in the picture should enhance that feature.

Walk around a favorite place. See how your shifting perspective changes the way the place looks in the viewfinder. What angle do you want? Do you want to show lots of sky or just a little? Do you want to move in close on a detail or climb high on a hill to show a broad expanse?

Adding a third dimension can be especially important in photographing landscapes. Include material in the foreground to help emphasize the distance of objects in the background. Late afternoon light can add long shadows that help define shapes and emphasize depth. Try to include something in the foreground for scale. Look for lines on the landscape (fences, hedgerows, roads, plowed fields) that lead the eye into the scene. Fill the frame, making every detail count. The whole picture, edge to edge, is important.

Light changes quickly at sunrise and sunset. So be ready, or you'll miss the magic of the moment.

Landscapes seem unchanging, but of course they're not. They change with the time of day, the weather, and the seasons. It's just as important to capture the best moment when you photograph a landscape as it is when you take pictures of people.

Boab tree, Australian outback

TIP FROM THE PRO

When you photograph a landscape, think about three things: What is the scene's most unique element? What is the best example of that element? What are the best lighting or atmospheric conditions for photographing that element? This landscape with a boab tree is an excellent example of how I dealt with all three of these elements.

SAM ABELL

"Develop a relationship with the landscape. Watch it change and evolve."

The Australian outback is Sam Abell's favorite place. It is "his" landscape; the boab tree is its most unique feature. He looked at thousands of specimens before choosing this particular tree. He found it during the dry season. Day after day there were no clouds and only harsh light. So he made a date with himself and the tree to come back in the rainy season.

"One afternoon a very dramatic storm came up, with strong late-afternoon light. I drove as fast as I could in the direction of the boab tree to get there before the sun set. But the light along the way was so amazing that I stopped twice to take pictures. I thought I had enough time, but I was wrong. When I got to the ancient tree, the sun had set. I was disconsolate and sat on top of my truck in despair, as the light grew dimmer and duller. Then, mysteriously, the light began to warm up. I looked behind me and saw that light from the sun was striking an enormous cumulus cloud. The golden light from that reflection was illuminating the land. I began to photograph the tree in this radiant light."

TRAVEL

To preserve the thrill of watching a fire-eater long after your trip is over, get as close as possible or use a zoom lens so you can eliminate distractions from the frame.

Travel pictures are really a combination of landscapes and portraits. They include the places you've been, the people you met along the way, and the people who traveled with you.

Go ahead and take the "classic" postcard pictures, then concentrate on taking pictures that reflect scenes the way you see them. What's happening around you may give you a new anglc on an old scene. Let's say you're at the Grand Canyon. The panoramic view is beautiful, but what really catches your attention is a group of tourists riding burros single file down a narrow path into the gorge. Focus on the riders, and let them lead you into the landscape. The result could be a photograph that highlights the grandness of the canyon in a very memorable way.

Vacations can be a good time to experiment with different camera formats. Try a disposable panoramic camera to photograph a very wide subject, such as Niagara Falls, or a very tall subject, such as the Empire State Building.

Flash

Airport X-ray machines can sometimes damage both exposed and unexposed high-speed film. Give your film to a security guard so it can be hand checked.

Jazz and New Orleans go together. This image captures this distinctive music and the historic architecture of the city's famous French Quarter.

SPORTS

Many of the high points in sporting events—the basketball player dunking the ball, the gymnast reaching the top of her flip—happen in a split second. If you wait until you see the moment in the viewfinder, it will be long gone by the time you snap the picture. You have to learn to anticipate the moment so that you are pushing the button just as it happens.

This means that you have to know your sport. You have to know when the basketball player leaves the ground how long it will be before he's got the ball into the hoop. You have to be pushing the button on the camera at the exact moment of the dunk. Even when you know your sport very well, you'll have to practice a lot to get this technique down. You won't know if you've succeeded until the film is developed (unless you have a digital camera).

Photographing sports is all about capturing motion. You can capture motion as a blur with the background sharp by bracing your camera and using a slow shutter speed (see page 24). Or you can follow the subject with the camera, using a slow shutter speed. This is a technique called panning (see page 62.)

It is difficult to photograph field sports from the end of a playing field or from the stands. The action is too far away. Even if your camera has a zoom lens, it won't be long enough. So get as close as you can to the action. You can't cover the whole field, so pick a place on the sidelines. If there is a fence, aim the lens through a hole in it. This will keep the fence from interfering with your picture. Don't waste time trying to shooting action on the far side of the field. Wait for the action to come to you. For evening games, use a very fast (light-sensitive) film—ISO 800 or higher. A flash won't work at these distances.

The photographer intentionally left the net in this photograph to show depth. It also makes the composition more exciting.

PANNING

On pages 24–25 you learned that changing your shutter speed is one way to capture motion. Another technique is called panning. It creates a picture with a fairly sharp subject against a blurred background. Here's how it works: Pick any moving subject that's not too far away. If your camera has a shutter speed control, set it for a slow shutter speed, such as 1/15 or 1/8 of a second. Pick a subject that is approaching from your right or left and frame it in the viewfinder. As it moves across your line of sight, follow it carefully with the camera and at the same speed as the subject. Make sure the subject stays in the viewfinder. Snap the picture when the subject is directly in front of you. Do not stop moving the camera after you push the button. Follow through.

Panning captures motion by keeping the subject sharp against a blurred background. It takes practice to learn how to pan at the same speed as the subject.

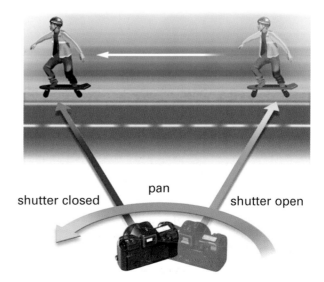

shutter closed   pan   shutter open

The streaked background makes this skateboarder appear to be moving even faster than he was. To achieve this effect the photographer used a slow shutter speed (1/8 of a second) and kept the skater centered in the viewfinder as he followed him with the camera.

Rodeo rider, Tucson, Arizona

TIP FROM THE PRO

Pictures are everywhere. Be selective. Pick your picture, then go to it and explore it. You can completely change a photograph just by bending your knees or shifting to the right or to the left. The best pictures are ones that ask questions without necessarily giving the answers.

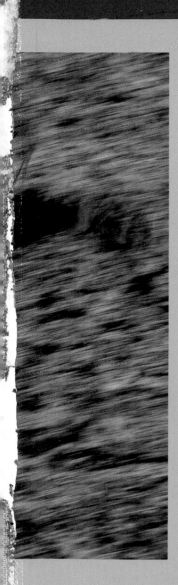

WILLIAM ALBERT ALLARD

"I love making pictures and exploring with a camera."

William Albert Allard admits to having a love affair with the American West. Growing up in Minneapolis, he always wanted to see the mountains and the plains that he read about in books and saw in magazines. The people, lifestyles, and places of the West have been the focus of much of his work.

This particular photograph was taken while Allard was working on an assignment about rodeos. "Lying back on a saddleless bucking bronco that wants to throw you to the moon is one of those events that truly run opposite of what I would expect would be a normal person's common sense. I took this with a telephoto lens from high up in the stands. I was following the rider, trying to keep him in focus, and snapped the picture just when the horse stretched out its legs in a powerful kick." By using a slow shutter speed and moving with the action, Allard was able to freeze the expression on the cowboy's face and keep everything else in motion. The result is an image that captures explosive action without losing its sense of balance and grace.

Allard uses his camera like a sketch pad, taking many more pictures than he uses. "I don't feel guilty about how much film I use when the failures are promising or interesting."

PICTURE STORY

A single picture captures a single moment in time. But you don't always have to think in single images. Sometimes a series of several pictures works together in a way that tells a story. Try telling the story of a sporting event, a school field trip, or a meeting of two friends. Let your pictures identify all of the high points of the event.

This series of pictures tells the story of hot-air ballooning. Clear skies, bold colors, and plenty of action make this a perfect subject for any camera.

Jane Goodall with chimp

TIP FROM THE PRO
Find the subject that really motivates you and go in that direction. If you want to photograph animals, spend a great deal of time observing them and learning about their behavior. Get completely familiar with your camera so that you can concentrate on the moment, not the camera.

MICHAEL "NICK" NICHOLS

"You don't just run around looking for pictures. You sit for hours to get one shot."

"Taking pictures is about looking. If I hadn't kept watching Jane [Goodall], I would have missed the chimp reaching out to her. I know Jane very well, so photographing her is like photographing family. She allows me to enter her world. In this particular instance we were at a zoo in Africa. This chimp had been caged alone for years. He would throw things at zoogoers. Jane, who has spent years living with chimps and observing their behavior, felt he was desperate for some sort of contact with other living things. She approached him with a bow, which in chimp behavior is a gesture of submission. I knew not to interfere or even to breathe. We were rewarded with this exquisitely touching moment."

Nichols considers research to be the most important part of an assignment. It lets you "hit the ground running." Sometimes what you see in the field is different from what you read in a book, but that's OK. You still learn something even though it may not be what you expected.

Digital Photography

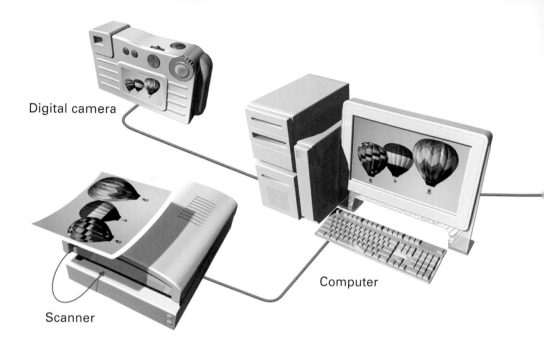

Digital camera

Scanner

Computer

D igital photography represents the latest technology in picture taking. With a digital camera you don't have to wait to have film developed to see your pictures. You can see them immediately on the screen at the back of the camera. You know right away if your pictures look the way you want them to look.

Unlike film, digital memory cards can be erased and reused. Because you don't have to worry about the expense of buying film and having prints or slides developed, you'll be encouraged to experiment. Maybe you're not sure if you have the lighting right. Go ahead and take the picture. Too dark? That's OK. Delete the image, turn on the flash, and try

A computer greatly enhances the use of a digital camera. It can store your digital images and transmit them to a printer or a friend if you are connected to the Internet.

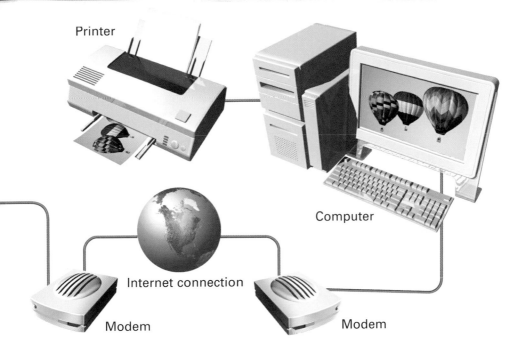

Printer

Computer

Internet connection

Modem

Modem

again and again. Then save only the best ones.

Some digital cameras can take pictures at different resolutions. The resolution of an image is the number of pixels (little dots of light, dark, and color) that can be captured in one shot. The more pixels, the sharper the image. But the higher the resolution the more memory the picture will take up on your memory card, your computer, and your e-mail. Your digital camera may allow you to change the resolution setting to high, medium, or low. If you're planning to send images by e-mail or post them on a Web site, use low resolution so the images will travel and load quickly. If you plan to print them out large, use high resolution for greater clarity.

This photograph was taken with slide film and scanned into a computer. The coach looks quite normal here (above), but look what happens when you re-arrange the pixels using computer software (right).

FUN WITH PIXELS

If you have photo manipulation software on your computer, the fun really begins. With the click of a mouse, you can change any picture that has been downloaded from a digital camera or scanned from a print or a slide. You can adjust the brightness and contrast, shift the color, take out red-eye, get rid of distracting things in the background, and even combine parts of different images to show something that never really happened or create something that doesn't really exist. In other words, you can use the software to show the world as no one has ever seen it or to make the real world look better. As long as you are doing this for your own personal use, for sharing with friends, or for doing a creative exercise, there is no problem. Go for it. Have all the fun you want. But, if you are doing a school paper or a project where factual accuracy is important, you will want to tell the viewer if you have manipulated any photographs. That way, you don't have to worry about misleading anyone.

If you have a photo manipulation program on your computer, you can alter the coach or any other image in ways limited only by your imagination.

AFTERWORD

Light from the fireworks makes the exposure. But you will need a camera with a setting that allows the shutter to be locked open until the bursts fade.

Photography is a combination of the technical and the creative, of science and art. The technical side includes light-sensitive film, microsecond shutter speeds, and shifting pixels. This book has only touched the surface of the technical topics. Far more attention has been paid to the creative side—to learning to think and see like a photographer.

The creative side of photography uses the vision of our brain and our heart as well as our eyes. Photography is about seeing something extraordinarily important or delicately small—something that only exists fully in that moment—and saving it. It gives us the power to create something that has only existed in our imagination. It helps us to see a familiar thing as if for the first time.

Take as many pictures as you can. Study them. Ask yourself why some work and others don't. Learn from your mistakes, but most important, keep shooting.

Go outside and look around. Look at the petals of a flower. Look straight up at the clouds. Look deep into the eyes of someone you care about. Seeing is what photography is all about. It is a tool to celebrate the simple fact that we can see.

There is beauty and meaning everywhere you look. Use photography to explore this rich and colorful world and share what you see with others.

RESOURCES

WEB SITES
www.nationalgeographic.com/photography
www.kodak.com/US/en/consumer/pictureTaking

BOOKS

_____. *Camera Basics: Getting the Most from Your Autofocus Camera,* edited by Peter Burian. Rochester, New York: Silver Pixel Press, 2001.

_____. *Photography, A First Guide.* Brookfield, Connecticut: The Millbrook Press, 1994.

Busselle, Michael. *Better Guide to Travel Photography.* New York: Watson-Guptill Publications, 1997.

Hartley, William W. and Bruce R. Hopkins (editor). *Loving Nature...:The Right Way: A Family Guide to Viewing and Photographing Scenic Areas and Wildlife.* Tuckerton, N. J.: Partnership Press, 1997.

Hedgecoe, John. *John Hedgecoe's Photography Basics.* Northampton, Mass.: Sterling Publications, 1996.

Kelsh, Nick. *How to Photograph Your Family.* New York: Steward, Tabori, & Chang, 2001.

Sadun, Erica. *Digital Photography! I Didn't Know You Could Do That....* Alemeda, Calif.: Sybex, 2000.

Varriale, Jim. *Take a Look Around: Photography Activities for Young People.* Brookfield, Connecticut: The Millbrook Press, 1999.

You will find the *National Geographic Photography Field Guide: Secrets to Making Great Pictures,* by Peter K. Burian and Robert Caputo, helpful as your photography skills develop.

GLOSSARY

APERTURE the opening in a lens that allows light to reach the film; see also f-stop

AUTOFOCUS a device that allows a camera to focus automatically on the subject in the viewfinder

AUTOMATIC CAMERA a camera that has a built-in exposure meter that automatically sets the lens opening and shutter speed

COMPOSITION the arrangement of everything in your picture—the subject, foreground, background, and surrounding elements

DEPTH OF FIELD the area within a photograph that is in focus

EXPOSURE the amount of light coming into the camera and the length of time it strikes the film or digital medium

F-STOP the number that indicates the size of the lens opening, or aperture

FILL FLASH flash that is used for adding light to dark shadows created by bright sunlight or some other bright light source

FILM SPEED the sensitivity of film to light, indicated by ISO numbers

FIXED-FOCUS LENS a lens with a focus that has been set by the manufacturer

FOCAL LENGTH the distance from the center of a lens to the film

FOCUS-LOCK the process of partially depressing the shutter release button to lock focus while you recompose

ISO the number on a roll of film that indicates film speed; the letters stand for International Standards Organization

LENS one or more pieces of glass or plastic designed to collect and focus light on a piece of film or digital medium

NORMAL LENS a lens that makes a picture look similar to what your unaided eye sees

PANNING a technique by which a photographer moves the camera at the same speed as the subject while taking the picture; creates the impression of motion by keeping the subject sharp against a blurred background

PENTAPRISM a five sided prism

PIXEL the smallest bit of information in a digital image; resolution increases with the density of pixels; the term comes from two words: "picture" ("pix") and "element" ("el")

PRE-FLASH the flash that goes off a second before the main flash to reduce red-eye in a portrait

RED-EYE the red cast in a person's eyes caused by the reflection of the flash off the lining at the back of the eye

RESOLUTION the number of pixels in an image; the more dense the pixels, the higher the resolution

RULE OF THIRDS in composition, the practice of placing the main subject off-center where imaginary tic-tac-toe grid lines intersect

SHUTTER the device in a camera that opens to allow light to strike the film or digital medium

SLR the abbreviation for single-lens reflex camera

TELEPHOTO LENS a lens with a longer focal length and a narrower angle of view than a normal lens; makes distant objects look closer

TRIPOD a three-legged stand for supporting a camera

VIEWFINDER the device on a camera that shows the subject area that will be recorded on the film

WIDE-ANGLE LENS a lens that has a shorter focal length than a normal lens and that includes more subject area

ZOOM LENS a lens that has an adjustable angle of view (shorter to longer and longer to shorter)

INDEX

Photographs are indicated by **boldface.** If photographs are included within a page span, the entire span is boldface.

Acknowledgments

Special thanks to the good folks at Dee's Photo Supply for their support and wonderful cooperation and to Megan Wooley for posing so patiently for all the studio shots.

Illustrations Credits

All photographs by Neil Johnson except: pp. 48–49 and 49, Jodi Cobb, National Geographic Photographer; pp. 52–53, Chris Johns, National Geographic Photographer; p. 53, Kent Kobersteen, National Geographic Society; pp. 56–57, Sam Abell, National Geographic Photographer; p. 57, Bill Luster; pp. 64–65, William Albert Allard, National Geographic Photographer; p. 65, Ani Allard; pp. 68–69 and 69, Michael Nichols, National Geographic Photographer; art pp. 7, 22, 23, 34, 62 and 70-71 by Slim Films.

The world's largest nonprofit scientific and educational organization, the National Geographic Society was founded in 1888 "for the increase and diffusion of geographic knowledge." Since then it has supported scientific exploration and spread information to its more than eight million members worldwide. The National Geographic Society educates and inspires millions every day through magazines, books, television programs, videos, maps and atlases, research grants, the National Geographic Bee, teacher workshops, and innovative classroom materials. The Society is supported through membership dues, charitable donations, and income from the sale of its educational products. Members receive NATIONAL GEOGRAPHIC magazine—the Society's official journal—discounts on Society products and other benefits. For more information about the National Geographic Society, its educational programs and publications, and ways to support its work, please call 1-800-NGS-LINE (647-5463), or write to the following address:

NATIONAL GEOGRAPHIC SOCIETY
1145 17th Street N.W.
Washington, D.C. 20036-4688, U.S.A.
Visit the Society's Web site: www.nationalgeographic.com